Jacob McDonald

A Treatise on Bee-Culture

Jacob McDonald

A Treatise on Bee-Culture

ISBN/EAN: 9783337330842

Printed in Europe, USA, Canada, Australia, Japan

Cover: Foto ©Lupo / pixelio.de

More available books at **www.hansebooks.com**

A TREATISE ON

BEE-CULTURE,

BY

J. McDONALD.

When the Creator placed man upon the earth, he put all living things in subjection under him, and said, "Have dominion over the fish of the sea, and over the fowls of the air, and over every living thing that creepeth upon the earth." He also established certain laws of nature, and gave man a reasoning, and inventive faculty, that he might discover the principles, and put them into use for his own benefit. The unalterable law of gravity has been made to serve him in various ways: in the construction of that wonderful piece of mechanism, the clock ; in the wheel that is turned by the effort of water, to seek its level, controlled by the same law, &c., &c. He has compelled the fickle wind to waft him safely to a desired destination ; he has applied the wonderful power of steam to do the samthing, besides a multitude of offices, and he has even chained the lightning and made it carry his messages from continent to continent. He has tamed the most savage denizens of the jungle and made them obedient to his will, He puts a bridle into the horse's mouth and leads him where he will, and of the fowls of the air, the natural instinct of the carrier dove, has been made to do man an important service.

Shall the "little busy bee" which indeed has been

tamed, still baffle the efforts of man to put it into complete subjection? There have been many systems of bee culture, and innumerable "patent hives," invented to effect this, but none of them has attained to perfection. The system explained in this little work, does not, however, claim absolute perfection, but it *does* claim to be an improvement that ranks higher than anything which has been heretofore attempted.

We would say in the first place, that to be successful in bee culture we must be able to carry over from one year to the other the work our bee does, together with the bees, without unnecessary loss. To do this we must know something of the nature and habit of the bees. If we have a proper hive we may do this, and the McDonald Hive is just what the common bee master wants.

1st.—It is simple in its construction and costs no more than a hive should cost to put bees in. Every bee master should have some little pride about what he puts his bees in when they will pay him well for all the money and labor he bestows on them. It has been said that there is no excellence without great labor but there may be great profit with but very little labor, if it is done understandingly in bee culture. We say there is some things that a man must know of the habits of bees if he makes the culture profitable; and there are a few things that he must do and they must be done in time, and at the time. The common method of colonizing bees is attended with much uncertainty and danger of loss to the bee raiser. Sometimes a colony will stay with the old hive two weeks longer than it should in the very best time for gathering honey, it then comes off and you put it in an empty hive; if the remaining season should prove unfavorable, it will die during the next winter; another one will come off and go to the woods and it is lost, and then the old colony will throw off some times as many as five colonies and they are not worth having, and while the old hive is weak from over-swarming, the miller takes advantage and destroys them. So you can see you must govern your bees or there is no success. Now if you will take the system explained in this little work, and adopt the McDonald Improved Bee Hive, you may meet all these difficulties and govern and control your bees the same as you do your horse, or sheep, or any other part of nature over which God has given man dominion.

The first that the bee-raiser should know is that it takes a Queen and fifty thousand workers to make a perfect colony of bees, and that it takes a box that contains thirty-four hundred and fifty-six cubic inches to contain that many bees, together with the comb necessary for that number.

The bee raiser must bring his colonies up to this degree of strength before he can either take stock or honey from them. You might as well say that a farmer can do his work on his farm with his two year old colts successfully as to say that the bee raiser can be successful in keeping his bees in boxes that will only contain a half colony. We say this is absolutely impossible.— Therefore to be successful we must conform to the above rule.

The McDonald Hive is made in two sections, precisely alike; each being one cubic foot inside. When these two sections are brought together, they make the hive above named. We make the hive in sections that we may have the complete control of our bees. As soon as a colony fills one section the other must be added; when both are full the bee-master may then proceed to divide his bees instead of letting them swarm the natural way. Directions for doing this will be given hereafter.

If you adopt the McDonald Hive and your bees are in good condition in the old hive you may let them swarm. We do not advise transferring unless your bees are in a bad condition in the old hive. If you th nk you will lose them; then, wo say, transfer them, directions for doing which will be given hereafter.

If the bee raiser uses the McDonald Hive he will have them ready, and as the swarm comes off hive them in it. One section is all you need, when-your colony first comes off but you must add the other section as soon as the first is full, as it takes both sections to make one perfect hive. Each section is made one cubic foot inside. Across the top of each section there will be eight bars or comb bearers. These answer a double purpose; one is to separate the sections, the other is to guide your bees in building their comb so it will be adapted to raising worker bees only. These are both absolutely necessary in successful bee culture. Thick heavy comb is only adapted to breeding drone bees.— Colonies often raise so many drones by having so much drone comb in the hive that they destroy the colony.— Drones are only consum ers and not gatherers of honey You will find by counting the cells in which drone bees are bred that there are only sixteen on one inch square, while there are twenty-five worker cells on one inch square; hence you will see the great necessity of giving your bees a guide to build their comb by.

The Queen carries a little sack in her hinder parts that is filled by the drone. When she puts her hind parts in a drone cell, the cell is large and does not fit her close, so when she passes the egg it does not touch this fecundated sack, therefore it will be a drone, not having touched this fecundated sack. When she puts her hind parts in a worker cell, the cell is small and fits her close and tight. She cannot pass the egg without its touching this sack; this fecundates the egg and gives it its sex. This has been proved by bringing the eggs under the magnifying glass. The drone egg has always been found to be a clear white, while the worker egg has shown a little streak that proves it has touched this fecundated sack. Queens have been dissected and this sack has been found empty in those that have not had connection with the drone bee. In others that have had connection with the male it has been found full, and as my aim is not to explain the nature and habits of the honey bee in full, only to give a few hints that will waken up an interest on this subject, I would advise bee keepers to purchase Langstroth's work on bee-culture, or some other work that has treated the subject in full, that you may be posted in

5

the nature and habits of that very interesting and profitable little insect, the honey-bee; and as my object in
this little work is to explain the McDonald System and
Hive I will try to do so in as plain and brief a manner
as possible.

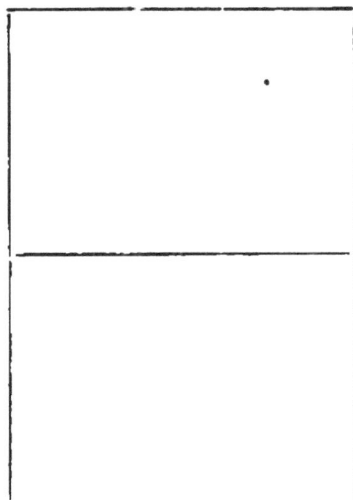

EXPLANATION OF THE SYSTEM AND HIVE.

In the above diagram we represent the double hive
ready to divide. The hive as it now stands on the middle of the bench, which is three feet and four inches
long, and one foot and two inches wide, is capable of
holding two hives, side by side. This bench has strips
tacked down on each edge one-fourth inch thick, one
inch wide, so that two sides of the hive will rest on
these strips. These will close the two sides and at the
same time raise the hive sufficiently to let the bees pass
in and out on each side of the hive This bench must
be placed so the bees will be free to form the habit of
working out and in on both sides of the hive. You
will find that about an equal number of the bees have
formed the above habit by the 20th of May.

There must be a cross board fitted in between the side strips three inches wide, and one-fourth of an inch thick. This will be tacked down across the centre of the bench to cut off the connection between the two sections when they are separated.

This bench may be made of an inch or inch and a half board by sawing off two pieces of scantling three or four inches square and one foot long.

Take the board above named and nail these two pieces of scantling securely across it about eight inches from either end. Bore two holes in each piece of scantling and put in good strong legs about fifteen inches long and you have the bench above described.— Bore two two-inch holes about ten in hes apart on each side of your cross board so that when there is but one hive on the bench, it will stand over both holes, and when you divide you will have one ventilator under each hive, for these holes are for ventilation. Now take two pieces of tin each large enough to cover one of these ventilators, punch them full of holes and tack them over the ventilators and you will have a bench ready for use.

The McDonald Hive is made in two sections. These will be made precisely alike. If you was making one hundred you would make them all alike. Take poplar or pine boards, dress them true to twelve inches wide, so that your pieces will be true and square ; this will make your boxes square so they will fit one on top of the other. You are now ready to saw it in pieces. You will need three pieces. Two of them will be cut twelve inches square ; the back will be twelve by fourteen inches ; the front will be made by dressing two pieces two and a quarter inches wide and fourteen inches long. These will be nailed on the front, one at the top the other at the bottom. You will fill up the sides with the same width this will give you an opening that will take in an 8x10 glass. You will put the glass on the inside by cutting a rabbet, the same as for sash.

At the top of the section there will be eight bars, or guides. These are made by taking an inch board ripping first into pieces one inch square then ripping them diagonally across from corner to corner. It will take eight of these bars to fill up the top leaving one-fourth inch space between them for the bees to pass from one section to the other. The bars are fastened in their place by driving two and one-half inch sprigs in each end, these bars will be cut twelve inches long placed inside the hive, at the top with the end to the glass and driving the sprigs through the hive in the end of the bars. You will then take your plane and dress off the top of the bars so your lid will fit down tight ou them, make a lid fifteen inches square of three fourth inch board, plain it bevel and fasten down on the top by driving in eight screws. It will not do to nail the lid down as you will want to take it off some times. You will need one lid for two sections.

You will now make your door to fit over the glass. Guage your door in one and one-half inches take it off one-fourth of an inch with your plane leaving it high in the middle. This will make it look like panel work.— Hang with small hinges and your section is ready for use except that you will need an aperture cut across the top of your lid six inches loug by three-fourths wide to let your bees pass up in the cap or honey box.

You will take your surplus houey by placing a small box over the aperture cut in the lid of your top section. that will hold from fifteen to twenty pounds of honey, This you may remove and empty as often as your bees fill it, after they have filled the two large sections. The comb and houey in the two large sections will belong to the bees for their winter store, aud to raise their young brood.

SYSTEM OF DIVIDING WHEN YOUR TWO SECTIONS ARE FULL OF COMBS AND BEES.

The 15th of March is the time to move the bees from their winter quarters, for we do not suppose that any bee master in this enlightened age will leave his bees to winter on the stand without any protection. Then we say the 15th of March is the time to place your bees on the bench, preparatory for dividing when the proper time comes, which is from the 25th of May up to the 15th of June. This the bee master's own judgment must decide, as it depends on the season and the condition of your bees. When the time comes and the bees are apparently numerous the bee-master will proceed to make two distinct colonies in the following manner: The double hive now stands on the middle of the bench and the bees having formed the habit of working from two sides of the hive, there will be about an equal number working from each side of your roof, (for you must protect your bees with a roof, directions for doing which will be given hereafter.)

In the evening between sun-down and dark you will move the double hive towards one end of your bench on the edge of your cross board. You will then close the fly hole so the bees cannot get out, then with a stick beat about three minutes on the lower section. The old Queen will pass from the noise to the top section. We suppose the young Queens will be in the lower section. You will then press a small chisel in the joint and break the clinches, then lift the top section, place it by the side of the bottom section, one side resting on the opposite side of the cross-board and supply the lower section with a lid placing a flat stone on it to hold it in place for the present, replace the roof and the work is done for the present. We say this Hive will divide seven times out of ten. The common bee-master, if he adopts the McDonald Hive will have advantages that he can have in no other hive. You will notice your bees the next day. If the divide is a success your bees will be working as naturally as before you divided them all the bees that formed the habit of working from the east side will now be entering the section that is now east, and those that formed the habit of entering on the west will be entering the section that is west so you have two perfect colonies, as they were one perfect double hive when they were together by having a proper hive and educating them to do what you wanted them to do, without any confusion to them, or interfering with the natural habits of the bees. If the bees appear confused you have only to replace them and there is no harm done. You may try it over in a few days. If you are satisfied the divide is all right, in forty-eight hours after they have been divided, take two empty sections without lids, raise the two full sections, place the empty ones beneath and place your roof over them and the work is done for the season. Drive the screws in the lid, before you add your empty sections.

The roof adapted to the McDonald Hive is made by planting one row of posts five feet high and nine feet apart. Saw a notch, eighteen inches from the top of the posts and let in a piece of three inch scantling, four feet long, in the form of a cross This will bear up your roof. Make it in sections so you can move it when you work with your bees.

With the McDonald Hive you may put two colonies together with safety. In the fall you may have some weak colonies that will not winter, you can add them to a stronger, and thus save them over for the next season's operation. To do this draw the screws from the lid of the weak colony, remove the lid, take one table spoonful of alcohol, four of honey or sugar, (add a little water if you use sugar) mix in a tumbler with a spoon, pour it on the top of the bars and it will run down over the comb and bees. Now place the strong colony on top. The bees from the top hive will go down to lick up the honey and the two colonies will thus become mixed.— The scent of the alcohol will scent the bees and combs and they will merge and go together the same as if they had worked together all summer You will then have a strong colony ready to divide the next season.

If a colony die during the winter you have only to remove the lid, add a section with bees in it, and you save the comb over the next season. This is carrying over all the work the bees do without unnecessary loss. All this you can do if you adopt the McDonald Improved Bee Hive. You will see the greater necessity for this when you learn that it takes twenty pounds of honey before they can build one pound of comb, just as certain as that a hog must eat one bushel of corn to take on ten pounds of fat. Now, you see how valuable comb already made is to bees, then, we say, away with the idea that the comb must be changed every three or four years. You might as well say that a man will prosper better by burning up his cabin every three or four years. Our advice is not to change the comb short of ten years, and you may leave it even longer with perfect safety.

WINTERING BEES.

One thing is certain bees must have sufficient fresh air. They take in oxygen from the air and give out carbonic acid gas and unless this is allowed to pass off, and fresh air to take its place the bees are poisoned by it and die. Thousands of dollars worth of bees are lost annually for the want of fresh air. The McDonald Hive provides for this.

Bees must be protected, in this climate, in the winter from the sudden changes from heat to cold. A man in Iowa, says that he came to the conclusion that what was good to keep ice in the summer would be good to keep bees in the winter and he built him an ice house sufficiently ventilated, and out of eighty-five stand of bees that he wintered in it he did not lose a single colony.— Some of them were very weak, so that he did not expect to winter them over, and he says he lost the winter before forty out of sixty-five, wintered on the stand without any protection. This house he says cost him forty dollars but, you say, we cannot afford to go to that expense for a few stand of bees. We grant all that but this need not hinder you from adopting some cheaper plan.

In using the McDonald Hive and bench, late in the fall, in the first cold spell, when the bees will have no disposition to fly, we place our benches about six inches apart, one double hive on each bench with the back of the hive to the south east, and the front to the north west. We then take hay or good straw, press it in between the hives and on the back, and then take fodder and tie it up in sheaves and set them up close together on the back of the hives. This protects the bees from the rays of the sun and keeps a regular temperature in the hives and the bees are not tempted out when it is too cold for them. There are more bees lost in winter from the heat of the sun than from the cold.

The back edge of the hive will rest on the crossboard on your bench. This will close the hive at the back.— You will now close the front so as to leave about two inches for your bees to work out at but so small that a mouse can not get in. You will have your ventilator in your bench all right, then place an empty cap over the aperture in the lid of the hive, with a small wedge under the side so some air will pass in and out. You will now set fodder in front, bound in sheaves, being careful to have one sheaf right in front of each hive so you can take it down to give your bees egress and ingress when the temperature is warm enough for your bees to fly, placing it back when it is cold. This, I think, is a very good and cheap way to winter bees in the climate of Ohio. The bee keeper should notice his bees every two or three weeks through the winter.

FEEDING BEES.

We say this may be done, but we never try to bring weak colony through the winter if we can add them to a strong one in the fall. This you may do with the Mc-Donald Hive, but when we do feed, we do it in the following manner. Take strained or inferior honey or the best of sugar, run it into molasses, boil and skim it then bake a loaf of corn bread one and one-half inches thick, split it through the middle, bake with some salt, and no grease. Then pour your molasses on the bread place it on a plate, put it under the bees so the comb will touch the bread and close your hives to prevent robbers from carrying it away. This should be attended to in the fall so that the bees may save their honey for the cold weather in the winter and be sure to attend to it in the spring for there are many weak colonies lost by neglect at that season.

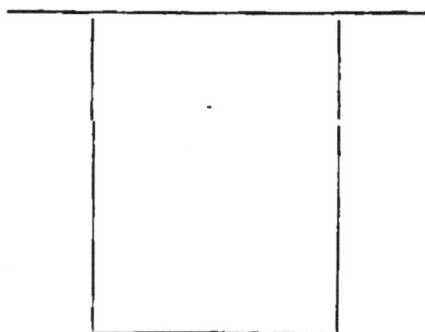

SYSTEM OF TRANSFERRING.

The above cut represents a frame necessary for transferring a part of the comb and honey with the bees.— This frame is attached to the bar that goes across the top of the section, it will be eight inches wide and eleven inches long one-fourth of an inch thick and one inch wide. The sharp corner of your bar may be taken off inside the frame. Drive a sprig through the bar in the ends of the sides of your frame, put a piece across the bottom and you have the frame you need. Fasten in the top of the section by driving in a one and one-fourth screw instead of the sprig as in the common section. Transferring should be done only in April, if the swarm is strong but later in the season if the colony be a weak one.

Take up the hive to be transferred, and place it upside down, some distance from its original position, place another box where it stood to catch the bees that are out; then have a box of the same size as the hive from which the bees are to be removed, and place it upon the top of the hive, month to month; tie a cloth around the two where they join to prevent any bees

13

from flying out, then with a stick gently beat upon the box containing the bees, about twenty minutes, when it will be found that nearly all of the bees have gone into the upper box. Remove the box now containing the bees, and place it on the old stand. Now carefully remove the combs from the hive, and selecting those which contain the worker brood, (the combs containing the drone brood, are easily distinguished by their cells being larger than the cells in which the working bees are bred,) with a sharp knife, cut the combs as near as possible the size of the frames, press them in carefully with the hand, and fasten in place by tying a piece of twine or tape around the frames. Then place the frames in the new hive in order, being careful to have the same edge of the comb upward as was up in the hive from whence they were taken. Now place the hive in its proper position upon the alighting board, take up the hive containing the bees, and with a quick jerk, shake them upon the alighting board by the side of the hive. This side of the hive may be lifted a little, a few of the bees placed at the entrance, and in a few minutes all of them will have entered. Screw down your lid and place the hive where the old hive stood.

SOCIAL ORGANIZATION.

Bees are never known to live in a solitary state.— They proceed upon the principle that it is not good for them to be alone. In this respect they differ widely in their habits from the wasp, the hornet and various kinds of flies. There is a reason for this which I do not recollect to have seen stated. The material which is used in the construction of their nests or cells, is different from that which is employed for the same purpose, by solitary insects, and this material cannot be used except at a high degree of temperature. The instruments to be employed in comb-building are small, and the wax must be softened in order that it may be spread. A solitary bee cannot come and deposit his quantum of wax, and thus enlarge the cell. The degree of warmth which is necessary for comb-building, is produced by the clustering together of the bees.— Their animal heat, when they collect together in a mass is sufficient for this purpose. Hence we are able to understand why it is they cluster very compactly together and remain quiet for the most part for several days after swarming, when the foundations are to be laid, and comb is to be built in their new home. The comb is built the most rapidly during the night, when all are at home, because the temperature is then the highest, or the animal heat is the greatest. It is observed that the temperature of the hive is at a higher point during the season of comb-building, than at any other time.— The naked hand placed upon the glass will be sufficient to convince any one of the fact, without the aid of a thermometer. They have the power of increasing or concentrating their own animal heat whenever it is necessary for the purposes just specified.

MEMBERS OF THE FAMILY.

A colony or swarm of Bees is composed of the Queen, the Workers, and the Drones. Each has distinct offices to fulfill, and all are important in their bearing upon the welfare of the society, or body politic which they form. They never revolt. They remain true to their organization, until death separates them.

The Queen is the mother of the whole family, of which she by instinct and by common consent is constituted the head. She is distinguished from the other bees both by her shape, color, and size. She is larger every way than the common worker, and longer even than the drone, and different in her proportions from either. The rings of the abdomen are less fully developed, or less visible. She has a more delicate structure than the drone, is more wasp-like in her appearance, with an abdomen more nicely tapered, or pointed at its extremity. She is of a darker color upon the back, especially upon the back part of the abdomen, than either the worker or drone. Upon the lower side of the abdomen she presents a yellowish, or semi-orange appearance. Her wings, when compared with those of the worker or drone, are wider, stouter, and shorter, in proportion to the length of her body. She is seldom on the wing, and is seldom seen except at the time of swarming, and when she comes forth in the open air to be impregnated by the males. She lays all the eggs from which the increase of the colony proceeds. The number of eggs which she deposits in the cells during a single season is truly astonishing, amounting to hundreds and even to thousands in a single day, as may be witnessed by those who use observatory hives.

Whenever she is taken away or lost, there is no further increase of the colony, and gradually, as daily losses occur, the colony becomes extinct. Many colonies are lost annually from this cause alone. If, however, she is lost during the breeding season, when there are newly laid worker-eggs in the hive, the loss is repaired by the production of another Queen. The usual process is to destroy several worker-cells around a worker-egg, and construct in their stead a queen cell. I have known queen-cells to be partially constructed in an observatory hive during a single night, after I have taken the Queen from the hive. After the cell is constructed or partially constructed, the same course is pursued as if a queen-egg had been originally deposited in a queen-cell, and in sixteen days another Queen is produced and takes the place of the one which is lost.

This result is secured because the worker is of the same sex as the Queen, and all that is wanting to render it a propagating female is a proper development.

The workers are so called because they perform all the labor of the colony. They seem to have no other propensity except to labor in various ways and to accumulate stores for the subsistence of the family, and such is their propensity in this direction that they often accumulate much more than is needful for their own supplies, and are able, and, I doubt not, are willing to furnish a liberal quantum of honey to their keeper to defray their necessary expenses, such as house-rent and the time which is bestowed upon them. They uni-

formly pay better for a good tenement than for a poor
·one. They like to work to advantage, aud never like
to be in debt, and if they are, it is not so much their
fault as that of the keeper, who fails to place them in
favorable circumstances, in which they can give full
scope to their natural instincts. Their industry is pro-
verbial. Some are employed during the working season as sentinels, some iu comb-building, some in gathering and storing up honey, some in nursing or feeding
the young, some in pasting over, masou-like, the crev-
ices and joints of the hive, some in removing from the
hive offending substances, and others like a kiud of
body guard, seem to bestow special attention upon the
queen. Whether the principle of the division of labor
is strictly adhered to by them, or separate classes of
bees perform constantly the same kind of labor, or
whether they are employed alternately or promiscu-
ously in different departments of labor, is a point
which is not satisfactorily settled by any observations or
experiments which have hitherto been made. Their
number varies in different swarms, from twelve to forty
thousand, according to circumstances, the size of the
hive or the degree of prosperity which they enjoy. They
are styled neuters, but are really females of dwarfish
size. The cell in which they are raised determines their
size. They are imperfectly developed in size, and their
female organs and propensities are in like manner imperfectly developed, because raised in a contracted cell,
except in some few instances. In consequence of a
more perfect development thau is usual, they have been
known to lay drone eggs. That they are really females
and not mongrels is proved by the fact that when a
queen is lost or removed from the hive in the hatching
season, a newly laid worker egg is taken from the cell
in which it has been deposited, and transferred into a
queen cell, which is prepared for the purpose, and by a
peculiar feed, called royal jelly, it becomes a perfectly
developed queen or mother.

The drone, like the queen and worker, is appropriately named. He is larger, stouter and more bulky than

the worker, and not so long as the queen. The drones are only males in the hive. They are hatched from April to July, and usually number from three to four hundred in a single colony. They are literally "gentlemen of leisure." They add nothing to the stores of the family, perform no labor, and do not even gather their own food, but live on the labor of others. They seem designed merely for propagation. Their days are very limited. When the work of impregnating the queen is performed for the following season, they are destroyed by the workers, who seem intent on carrying out the principle that he that will not work shall not eat. This general slaughter of drones usually takes place during the month of August, sometimes a little earlier. Rarely do they live longer than four months. None of them are allowed to survive the winter.

CLAIMS.

Bee-culture is an enterprise which has claims peculiar to itself. It is recommended to our attention by considerations which can appropriately be urged, relative to few, if any, other enterprises. It is both interesting and profitable, and when properly conducted, is conducive to mental and moral improvement. There is so much which is truly wonderful in the instincts and stereotype habits of the honey-bee, that the most stupid can hardly fail to be attracted by their curious economy, when their treatment or mode of proceedure is brought distincly to view, as may be done at any time by the use of an observatory hive. The inquisitive, the curious, the philosophical, and the refined, are, as a matter of course, most deeply interested in their operations.— There is too much true philosophy, and too much scientific accuracy in their work, to allow it to pass unnoticed and unadmired. The fact that their work pays a larger per centage of profit on the capital invested than any other is no slight commendation especially to those who wish to be paid for their pains, or wish to combine interest with profit. Those who engage in

bee-culture with a view to understand it must study and
think much, and this is conducive to mental improvement. It is an enterprise in which it is scarcely possible to engage without discovering the wisdom of the In-
finite One, and by those ideas which naturally arise in
the mind of the attentive observer, the heart, almost as
a matter of course, is made better. He finds

"Sermons in 'Bees,' and 'God' in everything."

Bee-culture has claims upon the *intelligent* and *sci-
tific.* *Professional men* should study the instincts and
wonderful economy of the honey-bee, that they may be
able to throw light upon their operations and thus aid
their less intelligent neighbors. It has claims upon the
sturdy yeoman as a kind of pastime, by means of which
he can reach ample profits with very little expenditure
of time and capital. It has claims upon the *young* as a
means of extending their knowledge of natural history
and cultivating within them the love of natural objects.
It has claims upon the *aged*, who, as they retire from
the active and busy scenes of life, need just such objects
of contemplation to occupy their minds. It has claims
also upon the attention of *females.* Mrs. B——, of
New Jersey, by her careful observations and economical
management, and valuable writings relative to the operation of the honey-bee, secured to herself a liveli-
hood, an education to her children, and gained much
celebrity as a scientific writer. Females are among our
very best apiarians. When the principle of domesti-
cation, which is found to exist in the honey-bee, is
properly understood, they will be kept on a much larger
scale than at present.

TESTIMONIALS.

CLAYSVILLE, P. O., OHIO, July 15th, '68.

MR. MCDONALD—*Dear Sir:*—I have divided three colonies of bees that I had in your Improved Hive and they work like a charm.·

JOHN HAWS.

CLAYSVILLE, P. O., OHIO, Aug. 2d, '68.

MR. MCDONALD—*Dear Sir:*—I divided three colonies of bees with your Hive and they work just as you said they would. E. KELLEY.

CLAYSVILLE, P. O., OHIO, Sep. 10th, '68.

MR. MCDONALD—*Dear Sir:*—I divided one of your Hives and they have done well considering the season. WM McKEE.

We the undersigned certify that we have been acquainted with J. McDonald who has applied and obtained letters patent on an Improved Bee Hive and that he has considerable experience in bee culture.—We have examined the hive and system believe it to be an improvement worthy the patronage of bee keepers.

REV. W. J. KEIL, Sr.
WM. E. KEIL, Jr.
THOMAS FRAME,
DAVID SECREST,
HENRY RHODES.

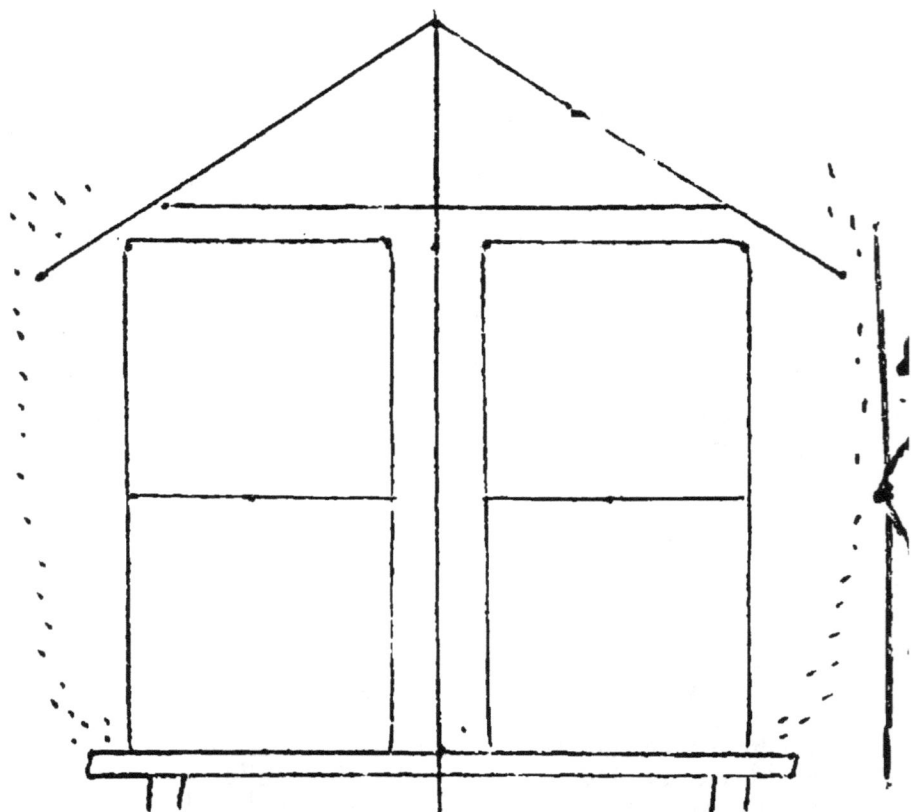

May 15ᵗʰ Divided & Emley Sections aded

www.ingramcontent.com/pod-product-compliance
Lightning Source LLC
Chambersburg PA
CBHW031158090426
42738CB00008B/1382